STEM-gineers

Pioneers in science, technology, engineering, and math

EXPERTS IN ENGINEERING

ROB COLSON

CRABTREE
PUBLISHING COMPANY
WWW.CRABTREEBOOKS.COM

STEM-gineers
Pioneers in science, technology, engineering, and math

Published in Canada
Crabtree Publishing
616 Welland Avenue
St. Catharines, ON
L2M 5V6

Published in the United States
Crabtree Publishing
PMB 59051
350 Fifth Ave, 59th Floor
New York, NY 10118

Published in 2019 by Crabtree Publishing Company

First Published in Great Britain in 2018 by Wayland
Copyright © Hodder and Stoughton, 2018

Author: Rob Colson

Editorial director: Kathy Middleton

Editors: Elise Short, Crystal Sikkens

Proofreader: Ellen Rodger

Designer: Ben Ruocco

Prepress technician: Ken Wright

Print coordinator: Katherine Berti

The website addresses (URLs) included in this book were valid at the time of going to press. However, it is possible that contents or addresses may have changed since the publication of this book. No responsibility for any such changes can be accepted by either the author or the Publisher.

Images:
t–top, b–bottom, l–left, r–right, c–center,
front cover–fc, back cover–bc
All images courtesy of Dreamstime.com and all icons made by Freepik from www.flaticon.com, unless indicated:

Inside front Aleksey Legkostupov; fc, bc Deviney; fcr Stedata; fcl, 14b Leungphotography; bccl, 14br Brooklyn Museum Collection; 3t Igor Netkov; 4b ShareAlike 3.0 Unported (CC BY-SA 3.0); 4-5 Jgroup; 6br Evolution1088; 6b Thomaseder; 6-7 Witr; 8-9 Shutterstock.com/cyo bo; 9tr Georgios; 10bl Johnsroad7; 10-11 Dmitryp; 11c Dennis G. Jarvis; 12-13 Shutterstock.com/iwonag; 13t Dmytro Adazhiy; 16-17 Rhodesfilm; 18-19 Adfoto; 19tl Arkela; 19tr Shutterstock.com/Zern Liew; 19b Sonulkaster; 20-21 Kmiragaya; 21tl Mxk; 21c ShareAlike 3.0 Unported (CC BY-SA 3.0); 22b Aneese; 24-25 Pn_photo; 25tr Halberg; 26b NASA; 27t Galina Balashova Archives; 27bl NASA; 28b Olena Ostapenko; 28-29 U.S. Navy photo/Ensign Dusan Ilic; 29t ShareAlike 4.0 International (CC BY-SA 4.0)

Every effort has been made to acknowledge every image source, but the publisher apologises for any unintentional errors or omissions that will be corrected in future editions of this book.

Printed in the U.S.A./122018/CG20181005

Library and Archives Canada Cataloguing in Publication

Colson, Rob, 1971-, author
        Experts in engineering / Rob Colson.

(STEM-gineers)
Includes index.
Issued in print and electronic formats.
ISBN 978-0-7787-5736-8 (hardcover).--
ISBN 978-0-7787-5822-8 (softcover).--
ISBN 978-1-4271-2233-9 (HTML)

        1. Engineering--History--Juvenile literature. 2. Engineering--Experiments--Juvenile literature. 3. Engineers--Biography--Juvenile literature. I. Title.

TA149.C65 2018   j624.09   C2018-905451-4
                                               C2018-905452-2

Library of Congress Cataloging-in-Publication Data

Names: Colson, Rob author.
Title: Experts in engineering / Rob Colson.
Description: New York, New York : Crabtree Publishing Company, 2019. | Series: STEM-gineers | Includes index.
Identifiers: LCCN 2018043637 (print) | LCCN 2018049448 (ebook) | ISBN 9781427122339 (Electronic) | ISBN 9780778757368 (hardcover) | ISBN 9780778758228 (pbk.)
Subjects: LCSH: Civil engineering--Juvenile literature. | Civil engineers--Juvenile literature.
Classification: LCC TA149 (ebook) | LCC TA149 .J66 2019 (print) | DDC 624.092/2--dc23
LC record available at https://lccn.loc.gov/2018043637

CONTENTS

THE ENGINEERING CHALLENGE

Civil engineers design and build structures such as bridges, buildings, and tunnels. Architects and engineers need to make sure the structures they design and build are strong enough to withstand forces, such as high winds or shaking from earthquakes.

The test of time

The Arkadiko Bridge in Greece was built more than 3,000 years ago for use by horse-drawn chariots. It formed part of a road linking the cities of Tiryns and Epidauros. The stone bridge has survived the test of time and is still used today.

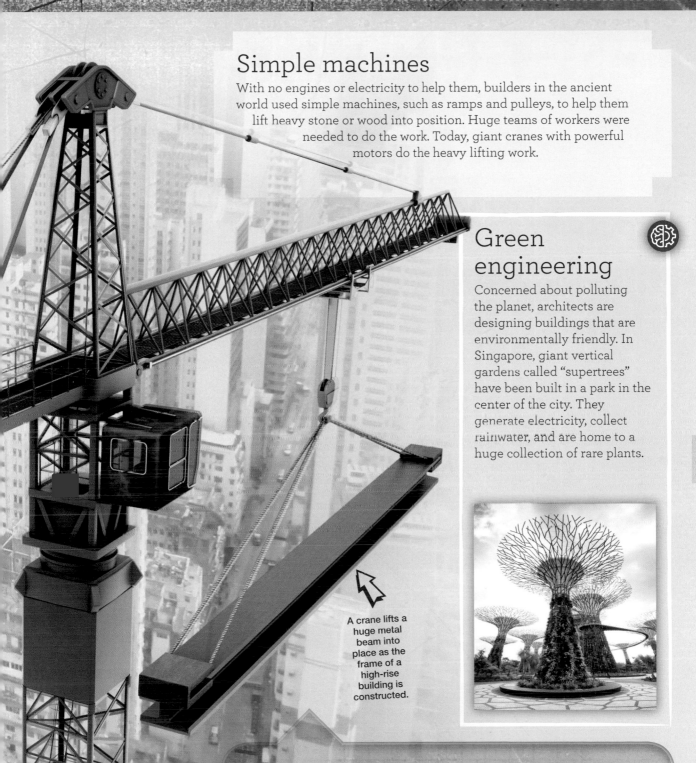

Simple machines

With no engines or electricity to help them, builders in the ancient world used simple machines, such as ramps and pulleys, to help them lift heavy stone or wood into position. Huge teams of workers were needed to do the work. Today, giant cranes with powerful motors do the heavy lifting work.

Green engineering

Concerned about polluting the planet, architects are designing buildings that are environmentally friendly. In Singapore, giant vertical gardens called "supertrees" have been built in a park in the center of the city. They generate electricity, collect rainwater, and are home to a huge collection of rare plants.

A crane lifts a huge metal beam into place as the frame of a high-rise building is constructed.

Read on to discover the challenges that engineers have overcome through the ages. The answers to each project's questions are found on page 31.

GREAT PYRAMID OF GIZA

The Great Pyramid was built in 2560 B.C.E. At 480 feet (146 m), it was the tallest of the three pyramids of Giza, in Egypt, and the highest building in the world for 3,800 years. It is the oldest of the structures known as the Seven Wonders of the World, and the only one still standing.

A square pyramid

The pyramid has a square base and four triangular sides that meet at a single point at the top. This shape is called a square pyramid. Before constructing the pyramid, Egyptian engineers had to level the ground to within a fraction of an inch in accuracy to create a firm foundation. They then began constructing the pyramid out of pre-cut blocks of stone.

Building blocks

The Great Pyramid is made from 2.3 million separate blocks of stone, each weighing about 2.5 tons (2.3 metric tons)—the weight of an Asian elephant. Some of this stone was cut from quarries 560 miles (900 km) away, and transported to the building site along the Nile River. The blocks were precisely carved, using copper chisels, to fit together along joints just 0.02 inches (0.5 mm) wide.

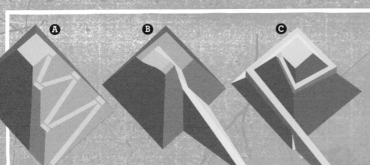
The ramps may have zig-zagged up one side of the pyramid (A), been built inside an incomplete part of the pyramid (B) or spiraled on top of the structure (C).

How was it built?

Historians still debate how the Great Pyramid was built. It is likely that tens of thousands of workers were involved, and that it took many years to complete. The stones were dragged into position along ramps, but we do not know how they were raised up the ramps, since the Egyptians did not use wheels or pulleys.

Burial chambers

The pyramids were built as tombs for the pharaohs (kings). The Great Pyramid is Pharaoh Khufu's tomb. Inside the Great Pyramid, three chambers, or rooms, have been found: a large chamber known as the King's Chamber, a smaller one known as the Queen's Chamber, and an unfinished Lower Chamber. In 2017, scientists discovered a hidden passage in the pyramid. What this passage was used for is still a mystery.

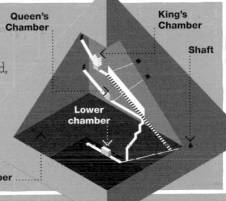
Queen's Chamber
King's Chamber
Shaft
Lower chamber
Subterranean chamber

The Great Pyramid stands beside smaller ones.

PROJECT: RAMP IT UP

The steeper a ramp is, the more force you need to drag an object up. Let's investigate this further.

You will need: a flat piece of wood, some books, a cup, a piece of string, an apple, and some coins

1. Make a ramp by resting the wood on a pile of books.

2. Attach the cup to the string and wrap it around the apple.

3. Hang the cup over the high end of the ramp and start adding coins. How many coins does it take to move the apple?

Change the slope of the ramp by taking some books away. How many coins are needed now?

LAYING DOWN TRACKS

Steam-powered locomotives were invented in the early 1800s, marking the start of the railway age. These heavy machines needed **parallel** iron tracks to run on. The first tracks to carry passenger trains were built in England in the early 1800s.

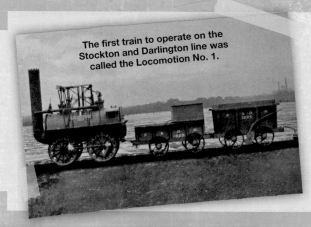

The first train to operate on the Stockton and Darlington line was called the Locomotion No. 1.

The first line

The first public railroad, the Stockton and Darlington Railway, opened in 1825. It was 25 miles (40 km) long, and trains took two hours to complete the journey between the two towns. Railroads proved very popular, and just 20 years later, more than 1,864 miles (3,000 km) of track had been laid across Great Britain.

George Stephenson (1781–1848)

Stephenson (pictured right) was an English engineer who built some of the first steam locomotives and railroads for them to travel along. For the Stockton and Darlington Railway, Stephenson set the gauge of his track (the distance between the parallel rails) to 4.6 feet (1.4 m). After the success of Stephenson's early lines, other railroads adopted the same gauge, and most railroads around the world still use it today.

‹············· **Gauge** ·············›

🧠 Expansion joint

When objects heat up, they expand, or get bigger. Iron rails heat up in hot weather. A gap of a fraction of an inch (a few millimeters) is left between sections of rail to allow for expansion. The clickety-clack sound is made when the train's wheels pass over expansion joints.

Expansion joint ·····›

PROJECT: HEATED NEEDLE

Explore expansion in action in this experiment. Warning: This experiment should be done with an adult.

You will need: a knitting needle, a cork, two bottles, a sewing needle, a candle, a straw, and a stack of books

1. Use the diagram to help set up your experiment. The knitting needle should be pushed through the cork in one bottle, and balancing on top of the second bottle.

2. Stick the sewing needle through the straw and rest the sewing needle underneath the knitting needle to form a cross, resting on the top of the second bottle.

3. Place the stack of books between the bottles with the lit candle on top, heating the knitting needle.

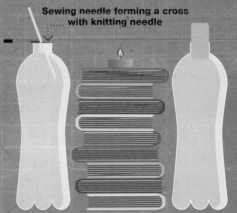

Sewing needle forming a cross with knitting needle

What happens to the straw as the needle is heated?

Magnetic tracks

The first trains were powered by steam engines. These were later replaced by diesel oil engines and electric engines. Today, maglev trains are powered through the tracks they run along. The trains hover above a magnetic track, known as a guideway. A changing **magnetic field** in the guideway can push the trains up to 373 mph (600 kph), making them the fastest trains ever.

WARNING LIGHTS

A lighthouse is a tower that sends out a beam of light to warn ships of hazardous waters or rocks. The earliest lighthouses were iron baskets filled with burning wood or coal, and mounted on long poles. The fires were replaced by oil lamps in the 1700s, and electric bulbs were used starting in 1875.

Augustin-Jean Fresnel
(1788–1827)

This French **physicist** invented a lens that multiplied the luminosity, or brightness, of lighthouse beams by four times. It was first used in 1823 in the Cordouan Lighthouse in France. The Fresnel lens produced a concentrated beam of light that could be seen 19 miles (30 km) away.

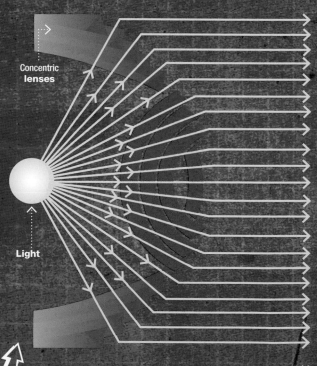

Concentric lenses

Light

The lens is made of a series of rings that refract, or bend, the light coming out from the bulb into a powerful beam of parallel light rays. Each ring refracts the light a little more than the ring inside it.

Keeping away

Lighthouse warning lights rotate to send a beam in all directions. This makes the light appear to be flashing when seen from a ship. Different lights rotate at different speeds. The frequency of the flashes helps the captain of a ship identify which lighthouse they are near. The light bulb used in each lighthouse has a set brightness, so captains can judge their distance by the brightness of the flash.

 Like most lighthouses, Cape Egmont Lighthouse in New Zealand is now fully automated. Until 1986, a lighthouse keeper lived there to maintain the light.

Range lights

Lighthouses can be paired up to help ships navigate the right course into a dangerous harbor. Called range lights, or leading lights, they are positioned in such a way that they line up one above the other when the ship is on the correct course.

11

PROJECT:
HOW BRIGHT IS THE LIGHT?

Measure how the brightness of a light reduces as you move away from it.

You will need: a flashlight, some books, paper, tape, measuring tape, and a calculator

1. Turn on the flashlight and place it horizontally on a stack of books on a table.

2. Place a piece of tape on the table along the beam of light every 2 inches (5 cm) up to 10 inches (25 cm).

3. Tape a piece of white paper to the side of another book, and hold the paper to the light at each distance. Trace a circle around each beam.

4. Measure the diameter of each circle and use a calculator to do the following calculation: multiply the diameter by itself, then multiply it by 0.785. This gives the area of the circle.

What happens to the areas of the circles as you move farther away from the light? If you double the distance, how many times bigger is the area of the circle?

Diameter

BORING A TUNNEL

The Thames Tunnel under the River Thames in London, England, was the first tunnel to be built under a navigable river, which means a river large enough for ships to use. The tunnel took 18 years to complete, and opened to the public in 1843.

Sir Marc Isambard Brunel
(1769–1849)

Brunel was a French-born engineer in charge of digging the Thames Tunnel. He invented a special iron tunneling shield that protected workers at the tunnel face. Once a new section of tunnel had been dug out, the shield was driven forward and the surface behind it lined with brick.

Brunel's iron tunneling shield was three storeys high and contained 36 chambers. Each chamber could hold one worker.

Tunnel-boring machines

Today, tunnels are dug using giant tunnel-boring machines (TBMs). **Hydraulic** rams press the cutting wheel against the tunnel face. A giant rotating head at the front cuts into the rock, and a conveyor belt at the back carries the rock away. For each new project, a custom-built TBM is made to the exact size needed for the tunnel. One of the largest TBMs ever made is nicknamed Bertha, and has a diameter of 57 feet (17.4 m).

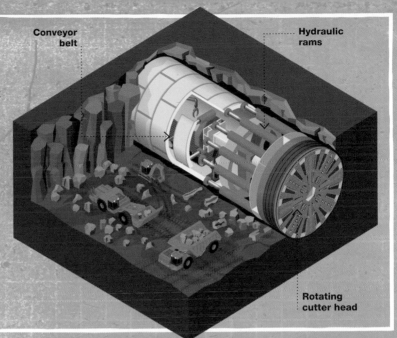

Conveyor belt

Hydraulic rams

Rotating cutter head

This is the cutting wheel of a TBM. It has cutters and scraping tools used to loosen material.

PROJECT: TWISTER

Let's investigate boring methods. Ask an adult to cut three slices of potato about 1 inch (2.5 cm) thick. Place the potato slices on a cutting board. The goal is to bore a hole through them.

You will need: a potato, straws, and a pencil

Try the following methods:

1. Push and twist a straw on the middle of one potato slice.

2. Jam the straw or pencil to force it through a second potato slice.

3. Plug the end of a straw with your finger and jam it through the third potato slice.

Which method works best? Why do you think this is?

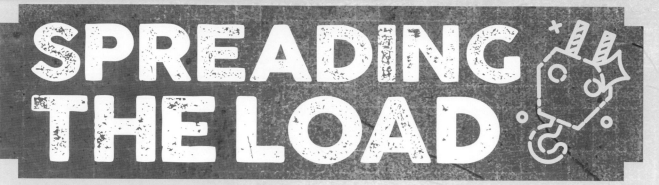

SPREADING THE LOAD

When designing bridges, engineers must consider the forces that put stress on bridges, such as compression (pushing inward) and tension (pulling outward). Different bridge designs balance these forces in specific ways to prevent the bridge from falling or collapsing.

14

John Roebling
(1806–1869)

American engineer John Roebling, designed the Brooklyn Bridge, a cable-stayed and suspension bridge, in New York. It was the first bridge to be made using steel-wire suspension. It is one of the oldest roadway bridges in the country, and the first steel-wire suspension bridge ever built.

The Brooklyn Bridge connects Manhattan to Brooklyn across the East River.

Suspension bridge

Cables are suspended between towers. Suspenders attach the cables to the deck, or the part that is traveled on, for support. The cables are under tension and the towers are compressed.

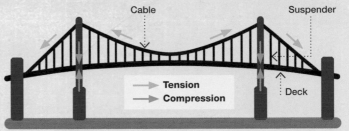

Cable · Suspender

Tension
Compression

Deck

 # Beam bridge

The deck is a straight beam that is under tension. It is usually placed on top of piers, or upright posts, that are under compression. Simple beam bridges with no piers are made to span short distances. The simplest form of a beam bridge is a log bridge built over a stream.

Deck

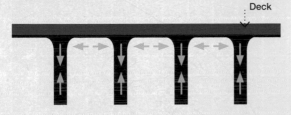

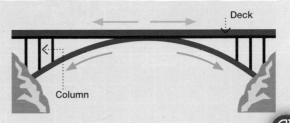

Deck

Column

Arch bridge

The supporting arch is under compression while the deck is under tension. The arch directs force to the sides. Arch bridges need strong rock on either side to support the compression of the arch.

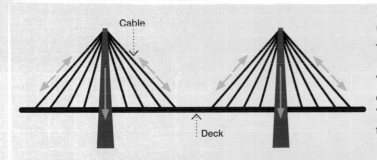

Cable

Deck

Cable-stayed bridge

The deck is supported by a series of cables attached to the top of towers. The cables are under tension while the towers are compressed.

PROJECT: TESTING BRIDGES

See how you can make a bridge deck stronger. Which bridge can hold the most coins?

You will need: two paper cups, coins, and three index cards

1. Suspend one index card between the cups. Place coins one at a time in the middle of the index card until it collapses.

Side view

2. Fold the long edges of second index card up about 1 inch (2.5 cm) on either side, making a channel when seen from the side. Place coins on top one at a time until card collapses.

3. Fold third index card lengthwise so it forms an accordion. Place on top of the cup, and put coins on top one at a time until card collapses.

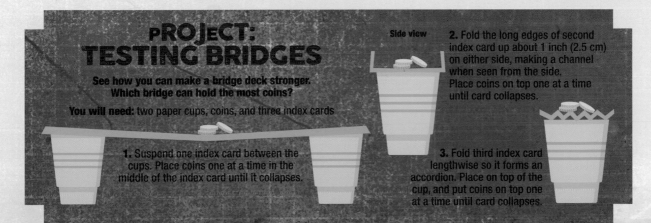

TOWERING GIANTS

Built for the Paris Exhibition in 1889, the Eiffel Tower is a four-sided pyramid made of wrought iron. The tower's strength comes from its frame, which is made up of **parallelograms** and triangles. Using a minimal amount of material, 186 triangles spread the weight evenly, making the structure extremely strong.

Gustave Eiffel
(1832–1923)

Eiffel was a French engineer who built many iron **viaducts** and bridges around France. He used his knowledge of the properties of triangles to make strong but light structures that would withstand the wind and rain.

If all the iron used to build the Eiffel Tower were melted down, it would form a solid block covering its entire square base, and be just 2 inches (5 cm) thick.

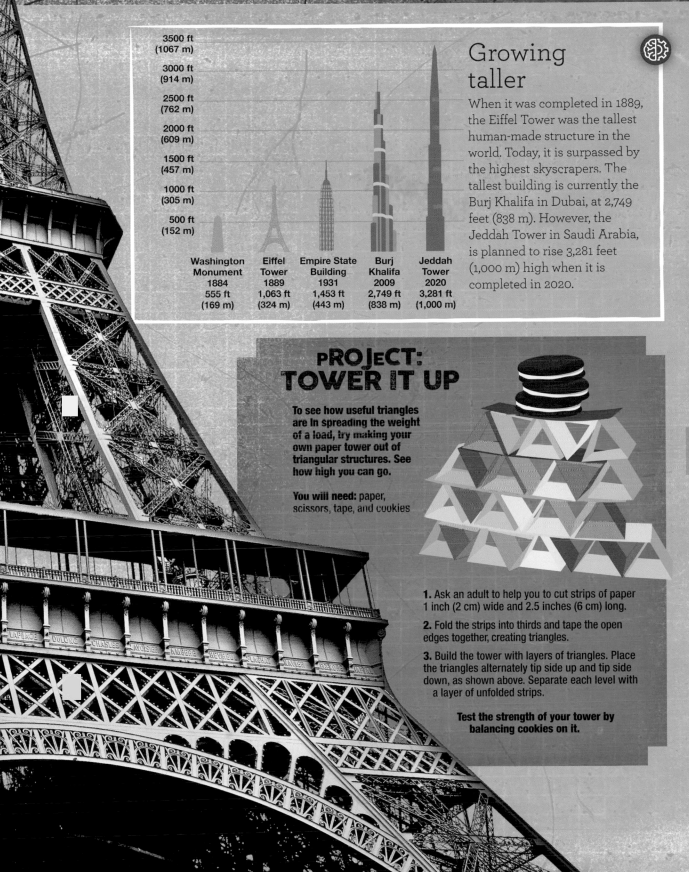

Growing taller

When it was completed in 1889, the Eiffel Tower was the tallest human-made structure in the world. Today, it is surpassed by the highest skyscrapers. The tallest building is currently the Burj Khalifa in Dubai, at 2,749 feet (838 m). However, the Jeddah Tower in Saudi Arabia, is planned to rise 3,281 feet (1,000 m) high when it is completed in 2020.

3500 ft (1067 m)		
3000 ft (914 m)		
2500 ft (762 m)		
2000 ft (609 m)		
1500 ft (457 m)		
1000 ft (305 m)		
500 ft (152 m)		

| Washington Monument 1884 555 ft (169 m) | Eiffel Tower 1889 1,063 ft (324 m) | Empire State Building 1931 1,453 ft (443 m) | Burj Khalifa 2009 2,749 ft (838 m) | Jeddah Tower 2020 3,281 ft (1,000 m) |

PROJECT: TOWER IT UP

To see how useful triangles are In spreading the weight of a load, try making your own paper tower out of triangular structures. See how high you can go.

You will need: paper, scissors, tape, and cookies

1. Ask an adult to help you to cut strips of paper 1 inch (2 cm) wide and 2.5 inches (6 cm) long.

2. Fold the strips into thirds and tape the open edges together, creating triangles.

3. Build the tower with layers of triangles. Place the triangles alternately tip side up and tip side down, as shown above. Separate each level with a layer of unfolded strips.

Test the strength of your tower by balancing cookies on it.

LINKING THE OCEANS

The Panama Canal opened in 1914. It cut across the country of Panama in Central America, and linked the Atlantic and Pacific Oceans. The new, safer route from ocean to ocean avoided the dangerous voyage around South America. First attempted by the French, the canal was eventually built by the United States. It took nearly ten years to build and required tens of thousands of workers.

John Frank Stevens
(1853–1943)

Stevens (left) was the American engineer in charge of designing the canal. The French had attempted to build a sea-level dam, cutting out a flat route. Stevens decided that it was necessary to raise the canal above sea level, and build a system of lakes and **locks** to carry ships along it.

A cruise ship enters the lock chamber at the Gatun Locks. ⟹

Panamax

The Panama Canal's locks could hold a ship up to a maximum size of 965 feet (294 m) long and 105 feet (32 m) wide. This size was known as the Panamax. Passing through this canal was so important to shipping, Panamax became the new standard size for all large ships being built. In 2016, a new set of locks set a New Panamax of 1200 feet (366 m) long and 160 feet (49 m) wide.

Up and over

The Panama Canal is 48 miles (77 km) long. Three locks at either side raise ships 85 feet (26 m) above sea level to an artificial lake in the middle of the canal called Gatun Lake. The lake provides a reservoir of water for use in the locks. It was made by damming the Chagres River.

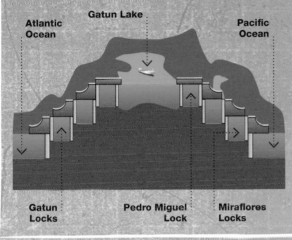

Atlantic Ocean

Gatun Lake

Pacific Ocean

Gatun Locks

Pedro Miguel Lock

Miraflores Locks

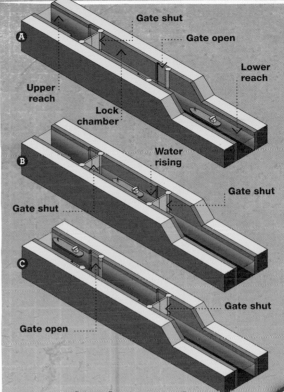

Gate shut

Gate open

Upper reach

Lower reach

Lock chamber

A

Water rising

B

Gate shut

Gate shut

C

Gate shut

Gate open

How locks work

Locks raise or lower ships in a canal. To move up a lock, a ship enters the lock chamber and the bottom gate is closed behind it (A). Water pours into the lock from above, raising the level of the water until it is equal to the level at the top gate (B). The top gate is opened and the ship moves out at the raised level (C).

PROJECT: MAKE YOUR OWN LAKE

Try making an artificial lake.

You will need: a large plastic container, sand, popsicle sticks, small stones, and water

1. Fill the plastic container with sand and dig out the path of a river from one end to the other.

2. Choose a place along the river, and build a dam using popsicle sticks and stones.

3. Make your dam a triangular shape so that it is stronger at the bottom.

Now test out your dam by pouring water into the river. To create a lake, the dam will need to let a little water through but not too much.

BUILDING HIGH IN THE SKY

The word "skyscraper" was first used in the 1880s to describe buildings with more than 10 floors. Now, some of the highest skyscrapers have over 100 floors. The oldest of these is the Empire State Building in New York.

The 102-story Empire State Building is 1,453 feet (443 m) high. It was the tallest skyscraper in the world for 40 years after its completion in 1931.

Steel frame

Chief architect William F. Lamb (1893–1952) chose a design in which the strength of the building was provided by a metal frame made from huge 44-ton (40-metric ton) steel beams. The limestone walls were hung from the frame. These are known as curtain walls because they do not bear, or hold up the weight of, any of the load. This is now the standard way to build very tall buildings.

The workers who secured the steel beams in place seemed fearless to onlookers. They worked with safety harnesses.

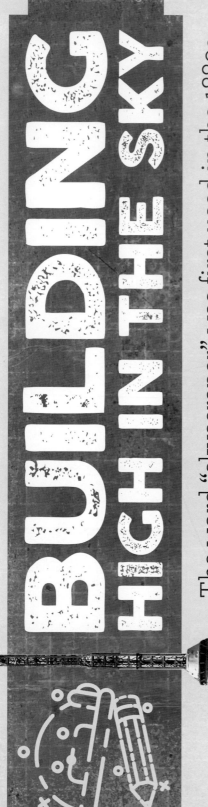

Downdrafts

Tall buildings such as the one on the left often create strong winds at street level. This is caused when air hits the building and is pushed downward. In New York, the Flatiron Building, built in 1903, became notorious for gusts of wind that would lift up the skirts of women walking past it. Today, architects test their designs in **wind tunnels** to avoid producing unwanted winds.

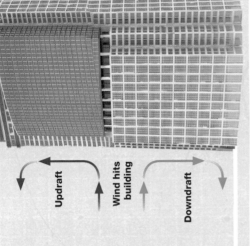

Updraft

Wind hits building

Downdraft

Mass damper

Strong winds are not just a nuisance at street level. They can be a danger to the whole building. The 1,670-foot (509-m) Taipei 101 building in Taiwan, withstands the effects of dangerous winds by using a device called a tuned mass damper. This 728-ton (660-metric ton) steel **pendulum** is suspended from the 91st floor. It sways to offset any movement of the building.

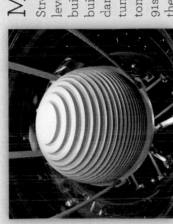

PROJECT:
LEAN ON ME

Some shapes are stronger than others. See how strong you can make a piece of paper.

You will need: paper, tape, and a pile of books

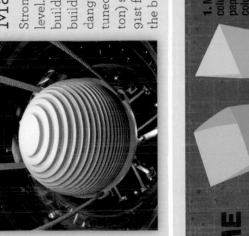

1. Make three different-shaped columns out of three large sheets of paper—a square column, a triangular column, and a cylindrical column.

2. With your columns standing upright, find out how many books you can balance on them before they collapse.

Which shape is the strongest?

HOLDING BACK THE FLOW

Dams are built on rivers to create **reservoirs** for water supply, to protect against flooding, or to generate electricity through **hydroelectric power**.

John L. Savage (1879–1967)

Savage was the chief engineer in charge of building the Hoover Dam. Working for the US government, Savage designed several other dams and canal systems in the United States. In 1947, he began work in China to dam the Yangtze River, but the project was abandoned. Nearly 60 years later, the Three Gorges Dam was completed on the same site, creating the largest electricity power plant in the world.

Hoover Dam

This 725-foot (221-m) arch-gravity dam was opened in 1936. It was built across the Colorado River, between the states of Nevada and Arizona. The dam created Lake Mead, the largest reservoir in the US. This 112-mile- (180 km-) long lake provides water to 20 million people. At the base of the dam is a power plant. Water gushes through its **turbines** at 87 mph (140 kph), generating enough electricity for 1.3 million people.

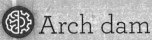 ## Arch dam

This concrete dam arches into the reservoir. Forces are transferred to the rock on either side of the dam. Arch dams are built in canyons with solid rock walls that can resist the pressure.

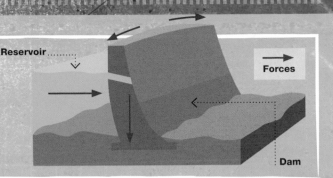

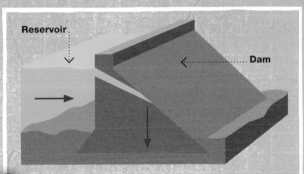

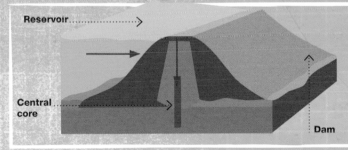 ## Gravity dam

These heavy concrete structures are designed to transfer the entire load of the water downward. They are often built across narrow valleys.

 ## Buttress dam

Buttress dams are similar to gravity dams but are reinforced with supports, or buttresses, that help to hold back the force of the water. The load is transferred both downward and into the buttresses.

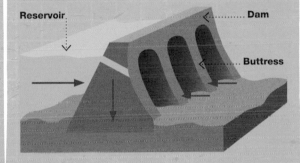

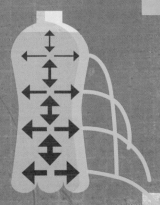

23

Embankment dam

Made of earth or rock, embankment dams transfer the weight downward. This kind of dam is often built for flood control.

PROJECT: UNDER PRESSURE

The turbines in a dam are placed near the bottom, find out why with this investigation.

You will need: 0.5 gallon (2-liter) soda bottle, a small drill bit, water, tape, and a bucket

1. Ask an adult to make four small holes, evenly spaced in a line up one side of the bottle with the drill bit.

2. Cover the holes with tape and fill the bottle with water.

3. Hold the bottle over a bucket or sink and take the tape off the holes. Water will stream out of the holes.

Which hole has the fastest stream of water?

POWER FROM THE WIND

People have harnessed the power of the wind for centuries using windmills. Modern wind turbines are much more powerful, and are used to generate electricity in a clean, **renewable** way. The first wind turbine capable of generating more than 1 megawatt (1 million watts) of power was designed in 1941 by American engineer Palmer Cosslett Putnam.

Turbine evolution

Putnam's wind turbine (left) had two blades, each 67 feet (20 m) long. It broke down after about 1,000 hours of operation and was never fully repaired. It was dismantled in 1946. A wind turbine of this size was not built again until 1979. Today's turbines have three blades, which are shaped to give maximum power. The curved blades are designed with a shape called an aerofoil. An aerofoil creates a force called **lift**, which pushes the blades up.

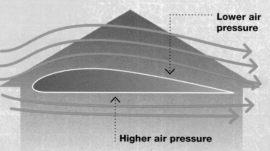

Lower air pressure

Higher air pressure

Air moving over an aerofoil moves faster than the air moving under it. This creates lower air pressure above the blade than below it, generating lift.

Wind farms

In areas with regularly high winds, wind turbines are grouped together into wind farms. The turbines in wind farms must be placed at least five blade-lengths apart so that they do not interfere with one another.

The London Array is the largest off-shore wind farm in the world. Located in the Thames Estuary near London, England, it contains 175 turbines.

25

PROJeCT: SPIN ME AROUND

Make a pinwheel turbine out of a piece of paper to see how wind blowing in different directions will spin the pinwheel in different ways.

You will need: a piece of paper, a ruler, a pencil, scissors, a skewer, and a hair dryer

1. Cut the paper into a square with 8 inch (20 cm) sides.

2. Fold the square along a diagonal, unfold it, then fold it along the other diagonal.

3. About 2 inches (5 cm) from the center, make a small mark on each crease. Cut along the folds to the mark.

4. With the skewer, make four holes to the right of each crease near the corners and a hole in the center.

5. Push the skewer through the center hole and fold each piece over so that the holes at the corners are all on top of one another on the skewer.

Use the hair dryer on a low setting to test your pinwheel. Make a prediction which way it will turn. Were you right? Which angle makes the pinwheel spin fastest? Is it more effective when you blow into the cupped parts of the pinwheel's blades? Can you make it turn in the other direction?

ZERO-GRAVITY ENGINEERING

Some scientists spend months living and working in space stations, such as the International Space Station. Space engineers face many problems when designing **modules** for people to live in zero-gravity conditions. Without gravity to hold objects or people down, everything floats. Simple things, such as eating and going to the bathroom, can be very difficult.

Tortillas are ideal food to eat in space because they don't create crumbs that will float away. In zero gravity, tables can be placed at any angle so that you can reach things more easily.

Space design

Russian architect Galina Balashova worked for the Soviet space program, designing the living spaces for the Soyuz spacecraft of the 1960s and 1970s. Her designs helped **cosmonauts** (the Russian word for astronauts) overcome the confusing effects of zero gravity. The ceilings were brightly colored and the floor was dark to create a sense of up and down. Balashova also designed deep zero-gravity bucket seats that are still used today.

Balashova made detailed colored drawings of her designs for inside the spacecraft.

Science in space

Scientists can find out many interesting things from experiments in zero-gravity conditions. Candles have been found to burn very differently in space. With Earth's gravity, the hot gas rises, pulling in cool air underneath it (see below, left). This provides a source of oxygen to keep the candle burning. With no gravity, the hot gas does not rise, so the candle burns slowly with a small, round flame (below, right). Engineers study how different fuels burn in space, and use this knowledge to design more efficient engines for cars or aircraft.

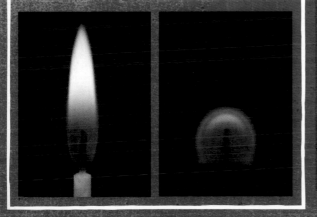

PROJECT: THE GRAVITY EFFECT

Astronauts in orbit still feel the effects of Earth's gravity, but their orbit is a form of free fall. Everything is falling at the same time, and this creates a feeling of weightlessness. You can see how this works very easily.

You will need:
a paper cup, water, pencil, and a bucket or sink

1. Using the pencil, poke a small hole in the side of the cup near the bottom.

2. Fill the cup with water, holding your finger over the hole. Let go of the hole over the bucket and see how the water pours out.

3. Now fill the cup the same way, holding your finger over the hole, but this time let go of the cup as you take your finger off and let it drop into the bucket.

What happens now?

GET READY FOR TAKEOFF

When building airport runways, engineers must take many factors into account. They need to build the runway to minimize the chance of dangerous crosswinds blowing across it. The runways also need to be as flat as possible, and must provide good grip for the aircraft's wheels.

Runways

Runways are given a number between 01 and 36 indicating the direction they are pointing. A runway 01 points toward **magnetic north**, 09 points east, 18 points south, and 27 points west. This allows pilots to line up their planes correctly as they come in to land. It is safest for planes to take off and land heading into the wind. To do this, larger airports have several runways pointing in different directions.

Planes can take off from and land on ships called aircraft carriers. The ship will always turn to face the wind. Pilots land by flying directly into the wind, knowing that the runway on the ship will be lined up.

Flying high

Altitude is a crucial factor when building a runway. It is harder to take off in thinner air, so the higher the airport, the longer its runways need to be. The Qamdo Bamda Airport in Tibet, sits at an altitude of 14,436 feet (4,400 m). Its runway is the longest in the world at 18,045 feet (5,500 m). That's 50 percent longer than required at sea level.

Runway on stilts

Squeezed between the ocean and a mountain range, Funchal Airport in Madeira, Spain, was one of the most dangerous airports to land at and take off from in the world. It had a short runway and hazards on either side. The runway was extended in 1986 by building a platform supported by 180 columns that were each 230 feet (70 m) tall. A main road runs underneath the runway. This innovative solution was engineered by a Brazilian company called Andrade Gutierrez.

pROJECT: PAPER PLANES

Planes landing into the wind maximize the force called drag, which slows them down. When making paper planes, you do not want too much drag because they will not fly very far. But you need enough lift to keep the plane in the air. The power of your throw gives the plane a force called thrust. Some of that thrust produces lift. Do research online to find ways to make paper planes of different shapes to see which will fly the farthest, and which will stay in the air the longest.

You will need: paper

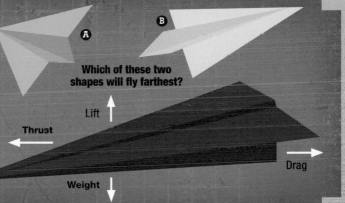

Which of these two shapes will fly farthest?

Lift

Thrust

Weight

Drag

GLOSSARY

ALTITUDE The distance a point is above sea level

CONCENTRIC Circles of different sizes that have the same point as their center

COSMONAUT An astronaut from the Soviet Union or Russia

DRAG A force that acts in the opposite direction to an object's motion, slowing it down

HYDRAULIC A system for operating a machine that uses liquid to transfer force from one place to another

HYDROELECTRIC POWER Electricity produced by moving water. The water powers turbines, whose spinning motion is turned into electricity by a generator.

LIFT A force that acts on an object in an upward direction

LOCKS Part of a canal that is closed off with gates in order to raise or lower a ship or boat, as it passes from one level to another

MAGNETIC FIELD The area around a magnet with the power of attraction

MAGNETIC NORTH The northerly direction in which a compass needle points in response to Earth's magnetic field

MODULES Units or rooms that go together to make up a spacecraft

ORBIT The path of an object in space around another object in space

PARALLEL Lines that follow in the same direction and never meet

PARALLELOGRAM A four-sided shape made from two sets of parallel lines

PENDULUM A weight that is hung from a fixed point so that it can swing freely

PHYSICIST A scientist that specializes in matter and energy

RENEWABLE Able to be used without running out

RESERVOIRS Lakes, often human-made, that are used to store water for use in homes, agriculture, or industry

THRUST A force that acts in the same direction as an object's motion

TURBINES Machines that turn pressure from moving water or air into spinning motion

VIADUCTS Bridges supported by a number of arches across a valley, river, or low-lying area

WIND TUNNELS Tunnel-like passageways through which air is blown to test the effects of wind on models of objects, such as planes

ANSWERS

p.7 Ramp it up

When you lower the slope, you should need fewer coins in the cup to move the apple.

p.9 Heated needle

As the knitting needle heats up, it expands lengthways. This rolls the sewing needle, causing the straw to rotate.

p.11 How bright is the light?

The same amount of light is spread out over larger areas as you move away from the flashlight. The area increases in size by a square of the distance. This means that the area of light at 4 inches (10 cm) distance will be four times larger than the area of light at 2 inches (5 cm) ($4^2 = 16$, while $2^2 = 4$)   [in metric ($10^2 = 100$, while $5^2 = 25$)].

[Math note: The area of a circle (A) is given by the formula $A = \frac{1}{4}\pi d^2$ or $A = 0.785 \times d^2$, where d is the diameter]

p.13 Twister

Plugging the end of the straw and jamming it through works best. Air is trapped inside the straw, keeping it stiff. However, air is a gas that can be compressed, so it allows potato flesh to enter the straw.

p.15 Testing bridges

The more evenly the weight is spread across the deck, the more weight it will support. The second channel-folded deck supports far more coins than the single sheet. The third accordion-style deck supports the most coins.

p.21 Lean on me

The circular column should hold many more books than the other two shapes. It distributes the weight of the books evenly. The square and triangle concentrate the weight at their corners, which then buckle.

p.23 Under pressure

The lower the hole, the faster and stronger the stream. There is more water above the level of the hole, creating greater pressure. So turbines are placed near the bottom where the water pressure is greatest.

p.25 Spin me around

When you blow straight at the pinwheel, it spins counterclockwise. If you turn the pinwheel to the side and blow into the cups, it will spin more quickly. If you blow into the backs of the cups, it will spin slowly clockwise.

p.27 The gravity effect

The cup and water both fall at the same rate, so no water pours out of the hole.

p.29 Paper planes

The dart-shaped plane (B) will fly faster. The glider-shaped plane (A) will stay in the air longest.